JOSE ALTUVE

Jon M. Fishman

Lerner Publications ◆ Minneapolis

Lerner Publications Company
A division of Lerner Publishing Group, Inc.
241 First Avenue North
Minneapolis, MN 55401 USA

For reading levels and more information, look up this title at www.lernerbooks.com.

Main body text set in Albany Std 15/22. Typeface provided by Agfa.

Library of Congress Cataloging-in-Publication Data

Names: Fishman, Jon M., author.
Title: Jose Altuve / Jon M. Fishman.
Description: Minneapolis : Lerner Publications, 2018. | Series: Sports All-Stars |
    Includes bibliographical references and index. | Audience: Age 7–11. | Audience:
    Grade 4 to 6
Identifiers: LCCN 2017002399 (print) | LCCN 2017012553 (ebook) | ISBN
    9781512450880 (eb pdf) | ISBN 9781512439236 (lb : alk. paper) | ISBN
    9781512456158 (pb : alk. paper)
Subjects: LCSH: Altuve, José, 1990—Juvenile literature. | Baseball players—
    Venezuela—Biography—Juvenile literature. | Baseball players—United States—
    Biography—Juvenile literature.
Classification: LCC GV865.A65 (ebook) | LCC GV865.A65 F57 2018 (print) | DDC
    796.357092 [B] —dc23

LC record available at https://lccn.loc.gov/2017002399

Manufactured in the United States of America
1-42136-25409-4/14/2017

CONTENTS

"200 PERCENT"

Jose Altuve gets a hit on October 1, 2016.

On October 1, 2016, Jose Altuve and the Houston Astros faced the Los Angeles Angels. The game in California didn't mean much for either team. The season was almost finished, and neither team had any chance of making the **playoffs**. Many fans watched the game to see Altuve do something special.

The Houston second baseman led the **American League (AL)** in **batting average**. Winning the batting crown is one of the most celebrated honors in Major League Baseball (MLB). With only two games to go in the season, fans wanted to see Altuve add to his lead.

They didn't have to wait long. In the first inning, Altuve came to home plate with no one on base. He quickly smacked a single to right field.

Altuve carefully watched the pitcher from first base. As the pitcher began to throw to home plate, Altuve took off like a rocket. He dashed toward second base. Safe! It was his 29th **stolen base** of the season.

Altuve winds up for the pitch during a game against the Los Angeles Angels.

In the seventh inning, Altuve came to bat again. He smacked another single to right field. Then he stole second base again. His 30th stolen base of the season tied him for second in the

Altuve sprints between bases during the first inning of the October 1 game.

AL. The Astros won the game, 3–0.

The Astros and Angels played their final game of the season on October 2. Altuve got one hit in four times at bat. He finished the 2016 season with a .338 batting average to win the AL batting crown. He also scored the league's seventh most runs, and his 216 hits were the most in the AL.

In November, Altuve was given two big awards. He was voted 2016 Player of the Year and the AL's Most Outstanding Player. Both awards are special because they are voted on by fellow players.

MLB players knew Altuve was a superstar. But the first thing many people notice about him is his height. At 5 feet 6 inches (1.7 meters) tall, he's shorter than most MLB players. In fact, he's usually the shortest player in the league. Most people assume his height was an obstacle he had to overcome. But Altuve turned it into a strength. "I knew [as a youngster] I wasn't going to be 6 feet (1.8 m) tall, so I have to always give 200 percent," Altuve said. With 200 percent effort, Altuve has become one of the world's best baseball players.

Altuve (left) stands for the National Anthem with members of the Astros.

Altuve is much shorter than many other MLB players. Albert Pujols (left) is 9 inches (23 centimeters) taller than Altuve.

Altuve's hard work paid off, and he played his first Major League Baseball game in 2011.

Jose Carlos Altuve was born in Maracay, Venezuela, on May 6, 1990. His father, Carlos, worked for a chemical company. Lastenia, Jose's mother, worked at home caring for the family.

Maracay, Venezuela

The climate in Maracay is perfect for a young baseball player. The average temperature is 77°F (25°C), and it stays warm all year. Jose played baseball every day. He and his friends played on fields, in yards, and in the streets of Maracay. When they couldn't find a baseball, they used a softball or a tennis ball. Anything that was round and could be thrown would work.

Many MLB players were born in Venezuela. Jose grew up with Kansas City Royals catcher Salvador Perez. Perez was sure Jose would be a great player one day. "He always believed in himself and I always knew he'd make it all the way to [MLB]," Perez said. "He works hard, he plays hard."

Playing every day helped Jose excel. He usually played **shortstop**. He was quick on his feet, and his throws zoomed across the field. At bat, Jose swatted balls in every direction. But his height was a problem for some **scouts**.

When Jose was 16 years old, he went to a tryout for the Astros. After the first day, two scouts told him not to come back. But Jose knew more scouts would be at the tryout the next day. Maybe *they* would look past his height. "[I feel like] I'm the same size as everybody else when I'm on the field," Jose said.

Houston finally saw that Altuve could be a star. In 2007, they signed him to a **contract** worth $15,000.

He went to the United States and began playing for teams in the **minor leagues** such as the Greeneville Astros in Tennessee. He worked on his baseball skills and got used to life in a new country. He also switched positions. Altuve played his first games with the Houston Astros in 2011. By 2012, Altuve was the team's starting second baseman.

Altuve prepares to make a catch during spring training in 2010.

Altuve keeps an eye on the pitcher as he prepares to steal a base.

During games, Jose Altuve gives 200 percent effort. He hustles all the time. He steals an extra base when the other team isn't paying attention. He focuses on every game and every at bat.

Altuve gets ready to play by giving 200 percent effort off the field too. In 2013, his batting average for the season was .283. He got 177 hits in 626 times at bat. Altuve knew he could do better. So instead of spending the entire **offseason** in Venezuela, he went back to Houston early. He was ready to work.

Altuve practices batting in 2013.

Coach Jake Beiting helps Altuve stretch so he can move quickly and easily without becoming injured.

In Houston, Altuve focused on three ways to improve: cardio, **agility**, and strength training. Cardio workouts such as running long distances strengthened his heart and lungs. He also played soccer. "When I don't feel like doing cardio or something, I'm going to go out there and play soccer with my friends," he said. Soccer is a good workout *and* a great way to have fun.

Agility drills help Altuve react more quickly at bat and on the bases. Short, fast runs and jumping exercises can improve agility. Baseball players also practice catching balls with their bare hands. This helps them catch and throw the ball more quickly during games.

Before games, Altuve practices hitting against a pitching machine. Then he takes dozens of swings from a tee. After that, he stretches, lifts weights, and practices fielding—all before the first inning!

To improve his strength after the 2013 season, Altuve focused on his legs. Strong legs allow a player to reach the ball more quickly in the field. They can also help a batter drive the ball over the outfield fence for a home run. Altuve lifted heavy weights in the gym and ran up hills to make his legs powerful.

Altuve jumps over teammate J. D. Martinez during a spring training session in 2013.

Altuve practices in a batting cage in 2014.

The hard work paid off in a big way. Altuve led the AL with a .341 batting average in 2014. In 2015, he hit .313, the third-best average in the AL. Then he was on top of the league again in 2016.

To stay in peak shape, he began to eat more healthful food. "[Altuve] learned how to eat," said teammate Javier Bracamonte. "In the minor leagues he was used to eating [fast food]. Now he stays away from junk." Altuve eats fewer hamburgers in favor of healthful options such as fish and rice.

Altuve's teammates run onto the field after Altuve scores in a 2011 game.

Altuve and his teammates love to dance.

You can check out their moves by tuning into an Astros game on TV. They dance in the **dugout** during games. If they win, they dance in the locker room after the game.

They have special lights and a disco ball to set the mood. Sometimes they even dance with fans on the field.

The Astros are a close group. When they aren't playing baseball or dancing, they're playing cards and singing and having fun together. "We're more than a team—we have a family," Altuve said. "We all get along great and that's really very important."

Altuve celebrates a home run with his teammates in the dugout.

Home in Houston

In 2013, Altuve signed a four-year contract with the Astros. He knew he'd be in Houston for a long time. So he and his wife, Giannina, decided to buy a house in the city.

Altuve, Giannina, and their daughter, Melanie, spend most of their time in the house. It has a pool and lots of room for a growing family. It needs to have a lot of space since family members often visit from Venezuela. Altuve's favorite room is the theater. He loves to watch movies there, especially action movies. He often watches alone, though—Giannina does *not* like action movies.

Off the field, Altuve rarely stops playing. He enjoys soccer, and he has a Ping-Pong table at home. Ping-Pong is a good game for someone with Altuve's quick hands. He also likes to play video games—especially baseball games.

Altuve's life isn't all fun and games. He also takes time to improve the lives of people in the Houston area. Working with the Astros, Altuve takes part in Community Leaders events. He meets with young people and helps them make healthful choices. At Houston's Urban Youth Academy, he helps children and teenagers learn to play baseball.

Every season, each MLB team nominates one player for the Roberto Clemente Award. The award honors players who have made a special impact in their communities. In 2013, the Astros nominated Altuve. He didn't win the award, but he continues to give back to the people of Houston.

MLB knew that Altuve was a special player with a special story. In 2015, they released a **documentary** called *Big Dreams: The Jose Altuve Story*. The movie takes viewers on a trip from Maracay to the major leagues with Altuve.

ASTROS RISING

Altuve plays his first game for the Astros on July 20, 2011.

The Houston Astros were a losing team when they called up Altuve from the minor leagues in 2011. They won 56 games and lost 106 that year. In 2012, they won 55 games. The following year, they won just 51 times.

The Houston Astros play the Kansas City Royals
in the 2015 playoffs.

As Altuve trained and improved, so did the Astros. In 2014, the team won 70 games. Then they won 86 games in 2015 and made it to the playoffs for the first time in 10 years. They were knocked out of the playoffs by the Kansas City Royals, the team that went on to win the World Series.

Altuve has had an incredible impact with the Astros after just a few years in the league. His 1,046 career hits already rank 12th on Houston's all-time list. Of the top 50 players on the list, only Altuve still plays for the team. He set another all-time team record with 225 hits in 2014.

The Houston Astros have never won the World Series. But the sky is the limit with Altuve leading the way. He knows what it takes to reach his dreams, no matter how big they are. "A lot of people told me that I wouldn't make it [to MLB], but every time they told me that, they encouraged me to show them that I could do it," he said.

Altuve has been to the MLB All-Star Game four times. He won the Silver Slugger award as the AL's top-hitting second baseman three years in a row (2014—2016).

Altuve swings the bat during a 2015 game in San Diego.

All-Star Stats

Jose Altuve has played only five full seasons for the Astros, but he already ranks as one of the team's greatest hitters. Take a look at where he ranks on Houston's all-time hits by season list.

Player	Hits	Season
Jose Altuve	225	2014
Jose Altuve	216	2016
Craig Biggio	210	1998
Jose Altuve	200	2015
Miguel Tejada	199	2009
Derek Bell	198	1998
Enos Cabell	195	1978
Craig Biggio	191	1997
Lance Berkman	191	2001
Carlos Lee	190	2007

Source Notes

8   Paul Hagen, "Altuve Big Winner of Players Choice Awards," MLB, November 9, 2016, http://m.mlb.com/news/article/208487348/altuve -big-winner-of-player-choice-awards.

12   Matt Snyder, "From Childhood Friends to AL All-Stars: Salvador Perez, Jose Altuve," *CBS Sports*, July 14, 2014, http://www .cbssports.com/mlb/news/from-childhood-friends-to-al-all-stars -salvador-perez-jose-altuve/.

12   Jerry Crasnick, "Jose Altuve Just Keeps Showing Up," *ESPN*, May 16, 2012, http://www.espn.com/mlb/story/_/id/7933839/houston -astros-their-very-own-little-engine-could.

17   Brian McTaggart, "Altuve Kicks Offseason into Gear with Soccer," MLB, August 18, 2016, http://m.mlb.com/news/article/196015580 /astros-jose-altuve-plays-soccer-in-offseason/.

19   Emma Span, "Little Big League: How Jose Altuve Became an Unlikely Batting Champ," *Sports Illustrated*, December 17, 2014, http://www.si.com/mlb/2014/12/17/jose-altuve-houston-astros -batting-champ.

21   Matt Young, "Astros' Jose Altuve Shares Importance of His Faith in God," *Houston Chronicle*, July 24, 2016, http://www.chron.com /sports/astros/article/Astros-Jose-Altuve-importance-faith-God -religion-8405832.php.

26   Brian Yancelson, "Jose Altuve and the Astros Are Winning—and Having Fun While They're at It," *Sports Illustrated Kids*, July 9, 2015, http://www.sikids.com/si-kids/2016/01/12/jose-altuve-has-astros -winning.

Index

Photo Acknowledgments

The images in this book are used with the permission of: © Bob Levey/Getty Images, pp. 2, 9, 10, 15, 20, 24; © iStockphoto.com/iconeer (gold star page numbers throughout); © Stephen Dunn/Getty Images, pp. 4–5; © Matt Brown/Angels Baseball LP/Getty Images, pp. 6, 7; © Dave Einsel/MLB Photos via Getty Images, pp. 8, 25; Jorgeprz/Alamy Stock Photo, p. 11; Mike Janes/Four Seam Images via AP Images, p. 13; © Brace Hemmelgarn/Minnesota Twins/Getty Images, p. 14; © Tom Szczerbowski/Getty Images, p. 16; AP Photo/Houston Chronicle, Karen Warren, p. 18; Juan DeLeon/Icon SMI CEM/Newscom, p. 19; AP Photo/Pat Sullivan, p. 21; © iStockphoto.com/jamespharaon, p. 22; © Denis Poroy/Getty Images, p. 27.

Cover: © Bob Levey/Getty Images.